TJ Plays Ball

Written By : Patricia A. Hill
Illustrated By : Sylvester L. Hill Jr.

ISBN: 9798366704748

AUTHOR'S DEDICATION

I dedicate this book to my family

Almond, April, Sylvester Jr., For believing in their mother when I said I would write a book about my grandson. Warren and Pearl, my parents, for creating me. The very inspiration of wanting to create my very own grandson TJ.

ILLUSTRATOR'S DEDICATION

I want to dedicate this book to my first nephew. His existence alone shifted my very own perspective of the world around me. Teachers come in all shapes, sizes, and ages. I want to thank my nephew TJ for teaching me how to be patient and look at things differently!

TJ PLAYS BALL

"Hello TJ, how do you do?
Grandma wants to play ball
With you!"

T
J

"Oh my TJ,
What a great catch.
You caught the ball!
Now can you throw it back?"

"Hello mommy and daddy, give TJ a try, throw him the ball watch how it fly! Great job, great catch. What a wonderful baby!"

"Football, bouncy ball a basketball too?

Nooo!! TJ not that ball, it's too big for a baby like you!"

"We can roll it, throw it ,
put it in a hoop,
  Up now down now loop
de loop!"

"Hello TJ, how do you do?
Grandma wants to play
ball with you!"
Yeah TJ!

TJ

Thank You for Reading

TJ PLAYS BALL

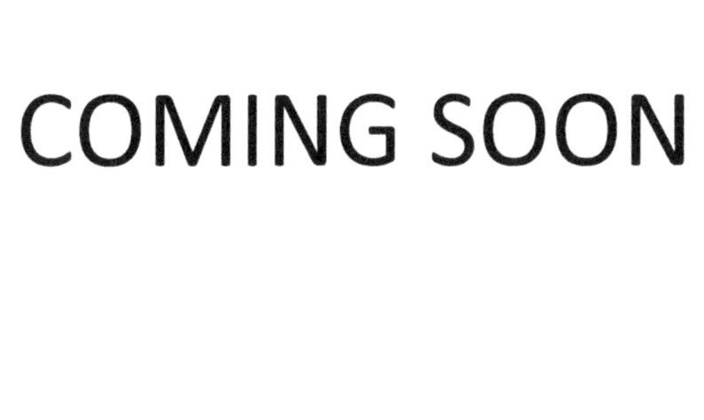
COMING SOON

Written By : Patricia Hill
Illustrated By : Sylvester L. Hill Jr.

www.ingramcontent.com/pod-product-compliance
Lightning Source LLC
LaVergne TN
LVHW071113160826
845679LV00004B/1061

9798366704748